Medgar Evers

by Genevieve St. Lawrence

Chicago, Illinois

For information, address the publisher:
Raintree, 100 N. LaSalle, Suite 1200, Chicago, IL 60602

Printed and bound in the United States at Lake Book Manufacturing, Inc.
07 06 05 04 03
10 9 8 7 6 5 4 3 2 1

Library of Congress Cataloging-in-Publication Data:

St. Lawrence, Genevieve.
   Medgar Evers / Genevieve St. Lawrence.
        v. cm. -- (African American biographies)
Includes bibliographical references and index.
Contents: Growing up in Mississippi -- The world beyond Decatur, Mississippi -- Marriage and a first job -- Working to end segregation -- The Jackson Movement -- Evers is murdered --   Evers' place in history.
   ISBN 0-7398-7028-9 (lib. bdg.) -- ISBN 1-4109-0318-4 (pbk.)
   1. Evers, Medgar Wiley, 1925-1963--Juvenile literature. 2. African American civil rights workers--Mississippi--Jackson--Biography--Juvenile literature. 3. African Americans--Mississippi--Jackson--Biography--Juvenile literature. 4. African Americans--Mississippi--Civil rights--History--20th century--Juvenile literature. 5. Civil rights movements--Mississippi--History--20th century--Juvenile literature. 6. Mississippi--Race relations--Juvenile literature. 7. Mississippi--Politics and government--1951---Juvenile literature. 8. Jackson (Miss.)--Biography--Juvenile literature. [1. Evers, Medgar Wiley, 1925-1963. 2. Civil rights workers. 3. African Americans--Biography.] I. Title. II. Series: African American biographies (Chicago, Ill.)
   F349.J13S7 2004
   323'.092--dc21
                                                      2003001511

Acknowledgments
The publishers would like to thank the following for permission to reproduce photographs:
p. 4, 58 Associated Press, AP; pp. 6, 20, 39, 40, 44, 47, 52, 55, 56 Bettmann/Corbis; pp. 8, 16, 24, 26, 28, 33, 34, 36, 48, 50 Library of Congress; p. 12 Corbis; p. 22 Flip Schulke/Corbis.

Cover photograph: Library of Congress

Every effort has been made to contact copyright holders of any material reproduced in this book. Any omissions will be rectified in subsequent printings if notice is given to the publisher.

Some words are shown in bold, **like this.** You can find out what they mean by looking in the glossary.

Contents

Medgar Evers sits at his desk in Jackson, Mississippi, in 1955. Medgar dedicated his life to fighting for African Americans' civil rights.

Introduction

Medgar Evers grew up at a time when African Americans in Mississippi did not have the same rights as white Americans. He worked to change the laws that forced African American and white children to attend separate schools. He helped African American people **register** to vote. Before citizens can vote in elections in the United States, they have to register, or sign up. But in much of the South, African Americans were not allowed to vote, even though they were citizens. Medgar also asked mayors and governors to hire African Americans as policemen and bus drivers. He gave his life in the fight for **civil rights** for African Americans. Civil rights are the freedoms that are promised to all U.S. citizens in the Constitution.

Medgar grew up on a small farm near Decatur, Mississippi. His father owned their house and a small piece of land in an African-American neighborhood. Medgar loved the open land where he and his older brother, Charles, fished and hunted.

Medgar Evers (far left) fights for civil rights as the field secretary for the National Association for the Advancement of Colored People (NAACP) in 1962.

In 1932 when Medgar was seven, he and Charles watched an angry group of white men tie an African American man to a wagon. The man had been **accused** of staring at a white woman. To accuse someone is to say the person has done something wrong. They dragged the man down the road and out to a field near Medgar's home. The white men hanged him from a tree and then shot him to death. They stripped off his clothes and left them in the field.

Medgar saw those bloody clothes every time he went hunting. He did not understand how these men could kill another man for a simple look. He also did not understand why the African Americans in Decatur allowed the white men to do this. Young as he was, Medgar knew that what had happened was wrong. He knew that African Americans needed to fight back and change the laws.

Medgar grew up to fight for the rights of African Americans in Mississippi. Some people were afraid of the changes African Americans wanted, and how fast they were happening. Sometimes, they beat or even killed African-American leaders. In June 1963, Medgar Evers was shot in the back as he came home from work. He died a few hours later. He was only 37. But the work he had done helped African Americans gain their rights. He is still remembered today as a pioneer in the fight for **civil rights.**

Medgar sat for this portrait when he was a young man.

Chapter 1:
The Family Farm

Medgar Evers was born on July 2, 1925, in Decatur, Mississippi. This area had small farms and thick forests. Medgar's family lived outside of town on a small farm. When he was not in school, he fished and hunted with his brother and with other children in the neighborhood. He loved living in the country.

Medgar was a slim, quiet child. He spoke in a soft voice and had a big smile. He loved to read and spent hours reading old books and magazines on his back porch. Sometimes, when he wanted to think about a problem, he kicked a can down the dirt road. He sat in the woods until he solved his problem. Then he kicked the can all the way back home.

A close family

Medgar was the third child of James and Jessie Evers. He had an older brother, Charles, an older sister, Elizabeth, and a younger

In his own words

"It may sound funny, but I love the South. . . .There is room here for my children to play and grow, and become good citizens—if the white man will let them."

From Medgar's 1958 essay "Why I Live in Mississippi"

"Tonight the Negro plantation worker in the Delta knows from his radio and television what happened today all over the world. . . . He knows about the new free nations in Africa and knows that a Congo native can be a locomotive engineer, but in Jackson, he cannot even drive a garbage truck."

From Medgar's last radio speech, May 1963

"[Jackson is] a city of over 150,000, of which 40% is Negro, in which there is not a single Negro policeman or policewoman, school crossing guard, fireman, clerk, or supervisor employed in any city department."

From Medgar's last radio speech, May 1963

"Freedom has never been free. . . . I love my children, and I love my wife with all my heart. And I would die, and die gladly, if that would make a better life for them."

*From a speech at an **NAACP** rally, June 7, 1963*

sister, Mary Ruth. He also had three older stepbrothers and stepsisters from his mother's first marriage. Even though Medgar's parents worked very hard, they were poor.

Medgar's father grew cotton on his land. He also raised cows, pigs, and chickens. Medgar helped his father in the fields and milked the cows. Because the farm was small, his father also worked in a lumberyard to make extra money. Every two years, James Evers took his children to town and bought two pairs of shoes for each of them. They wore the good pair only for church and funerals. They wore the other shoes in the winter. The rest of the time, the children went barefoot.

Jessie Evers grew okra, peas, corn, and potatoes in their garden. She was a good cook, and the family ate well. Jessie Evers sewed all the clothes for her family. She used cotton and flour sacks to make shirts and pants for the boys and dresses for the girls. Sometimes she sewed all night. Her house was always clean and neat. She was very proud of her home and her children.

Medgar's mother also worked six days a week for a white family. She got up before sunrise and walked a mile to work. She cooked for the white family, washed their clothes, and took care of their children. Jessie Evers earned 50 cents a day for this work. In the evening, she hurried home and cooked dinner for her own family.

African-American students sit at desks around a stove in a one-room schoolhouse in the early twentieth century. Medgar and his brother attended a school like this one.

Sunday was his mother's only day off. Every Sunday, the family went to church at nine in the morning and stayed until ten at night. The children went to Sunday school, listened to sermons, and joined other church groups. Jessie Evers also read to the children from the Bible every night.

Because both of their parents worked, the Evers children helped out as soon as they were old enough. The older girls did chores around the house and cared for the younger children. Medgar and Charles chopped wood for the stove, carried water from the stream, and fed the animals. They helped their father plant and pick the cotton. Medgar's neighbors respected the family because they owned their farm, and because they all worked so hard.

A one-room school

Black children could only go to schools set aside for blacks. Medgar's elementary school was three miles from the farm. The school was open from mid-October until mid-February. Black children were only able to go to school in the winter, when they were not working in the fields. Medgar and his brother walked to school every day. It gets cold and damp in Mississippi in the winter. The boys were always cold because they did not have good shoes or warm jackets.

Schools for black children rarely received as much money as the schools for white children. Only two teachers taught more than 100 children at the Decatur Consolidated School. The one-room wooden building leaked when it rained. Every morning, the Evers boys went out to get firewood for the stove. The children wrapped their feet in blankets to keep warm. The teachers taught the first through the eighth grade. They taught math, history, reading, and arithmetic. The school had very few books, and the books they did have were old.

World War II (1939–1945)

In 1939 Adolf Hitler and the German army marched into Poland. This started a war that became known as World War II. When Germany refused to leave Poland, Britain, and France declared war on Germany. The war spread across Europe, and into Asia and North Africa. The United States stayed out of the war at first. But in December 1941, the Japanese, who sided with Germany, bombed the U.S. Navy at Pearl Harbor in Hawaii. The next day, President Franklin D. Roosevelt declared war against Japan, Germany, and Italy, which also sided with Germany.

African Americans have served in every major American war, but they were **segregated** until after WW II. When Medgar and Charles Evers joined the army, they were kept separate from white soldiers. They slept in separate housing, fought in separate units, and were often treated poorly by their white officers. Charles was sent to fight the Japanese in the Philippines. Medgar was sent to fight the Germans in France.

More than one million African Americans served during WW II. Those who fought in Europe found that white Europeans treated African-American soldiers the same way they treated any other human being. Black people were not segregated or discriminated against there. But when these soldiers came home after the war, segregation once again kept them from going to good schools and getting good jobs. Many of these men and women helped start the fight for equal rights in the United States.

In 1948 President Harry Truman changed the rules that kept the military segregated. Now soldiers of different **races** are treated equally in the United States military.

Segregation

While Decatur's African-American children studied in a cold, leaky building, the white children were bused to a new school nearby. Some of the white children on the bus shouted names and threw rocks when they passed the African-American children. Like the other southern states, Mississippi had laws to keep the African Americans separate from the whites. This was called **segregation.**

Medgar could see that his education was not as good as white children's. The white children had warm classrooms and new books, and they rode a bus to school. When he asked his mother why the white children were special, she told him that was just life in Mississippi. Medgar looked forward to the day when all children in Mississippi could get a good education. He wanted African-American children to be able to go to any school near their homes.

In the 1940s, Mississippi schools were segregated. Schools for African-American children were often cold, leaky, and far away from home.

Chapter 2:
The World Outside Decatur

Many African-American children in Decatur quit school after the eighth grade. But James and Jessie Evers believed that education was important. They knew education would help their children find better jobs. The nearest high school for African Americans was twelve miles away, in Newton, Mississippi.

Every day Medgar walked to school and home again. It was a very long walk. He decided he needed a bicycle. He painted houses, mowed lawns, and worked on farms until he had enough money. The bicycle made his trip easier. But Medgar was angry about the long trip. White children went to high school right in Decatur.

Medgar joins the army

In 1943 Medgar quit high school and joined the army. He was seventeen years old. His brother Charles had joined in 1939, also at seventeen. The brothers saw the army as a way to leave Mississippi and see more of the world. It promised good pay and a chance to learn skills they could not learn in Mississippi.

In 1943 the United States was fighting World War II (1939–1945) against Germany, Italy, and Japan. Medgar's unit fought to take France back from the Germans. They landed at Omaha Beach, on the northern coast of France. More than 3,000 soldiers died or were injured the first day. Though Medgar survived, he saw many men die in battle.

After the battle, Medgar's unit stayed in northern France for more than two years. He made friends with a French family and they invited him to dinner. Blacks and whites never mixed this way in Mississippi. In France, though, Medgar saw whites and blacks living together peacefully. There, he was a soldier and an American. It did not matter to the French that he was African American.

During WW II, the American Army was **segregated.** All Medgar's officers were white, and many of them treated African American soldiers badly. But one white officer saw that Medgar was smart and liked to read. He encouraged him to go back to school after the war. This was the first time a white officer had showed Medgar respect. He began to see that life might be better for African Americans outside of Mississippi.

After the War

Medgar came home from the war when he was 20. After working for a year, he went back to school. The Army gave soldiers money to go back to school. Medgar took classes to finish high school. Although he was 21 and older than most high school students, some other returning soldiers were in his classes. With the help of a good English teacher, Medgar began to enjoy studying.

When he finished high school, he followed his brother, Charles, to Alcorn State College of Mississippi. Alcorn was a school for African-American students. He studied business, even though there were few business jobs for African Americans in Mississippi. At that time, whites encouraged African-American college graduates to become teachers. He did not know what he wanted to be, but he wanted to choose his own job.

Medgar was popular at Alcorn. He played football and ran on the track team. He was also the editor of the school newspaper and sang in the choir. He joined the Young Men's Christian Association (YMCA) and traveled to Millsaps College, a white school in Jackson, Mississippi, for monthly meetings with white students. The YMCA, like the Young Women's Christian Association (YWCA), was not just a place to swim or play basketball. Slowly, over the course of many years, it had come to take a stand against **segregation.** It did an important thing: It gave young African-American and white students in the South a rare chance to get to know each other.

These young people sing together at a YMCA party in Harlem in New York City in the mid-twentieth century. YMCAs gave youth of different races a chance to get to know each other.

When Medgar was a senior, he was chosen for Who's Who in American Colleges. This book honored the best college students in the United States.

Summers in Chicago

To earn extra money for college, Medgar moved to Chicago, Illinois in the summers. He and Charles drove an old car to Chicago and stayed near one of their older sisters. Medgar worked at many jobs in Chicago. He worked in construction and in meatpacking plants. The jobs paid well, and he saved money for the next school year.

In Chicago, African Americans could go to many of the beaches, the libraries, and the movies with whites. They could sit anywhere they wanted on buses and trains. African Americans had much more freedom in Chicago than in Mississippi. Even so, Medgar did not like Chicago. He thought it was too big and too noisy. He missed the open countryside in Mississippi. He did not want to move north. He wanted to bring the freedom he saw in the North to Mississippi.

Marriage

In 1950 a shy young woman named Myrlie Beasley came to Alcorn State College to study music. Myrlie had been raised in Vicksburg, Mississippi, by her aunt and her grandmother. She was seventeen and had never been away from home before.

On her first day, Myrlie met Medgar at a party at the college president's house. She saw a polite, serious young man. He was a star of the football team and president of the junior class. Soon, he began to come by to listen to her practice the piano. He told her he liked listening to her play. This was true, but he also wanted to get to know her. On Christmas Eve of 1951, Medgar and Myrlie were married in Vicksburg, Mississippi.

Medgar's wife Myrlie holds their son Darrell in 1963.

Chapter 3:
Graduation and a First Job

When Medgar graduated in 1952, he took a job selling **insurance** for the Magnolia Mutual Insurance Company. When people buy insurance from a company, the company pays for their doctor, hospital, or funeral bills. The company was owned by an African American, and many students at Alcorn State College wanted to work there. Businesses owned by whites did not hire African Americans for sales jobs.

Medgar and Myrlie moved to the African-American community of Mound Bayou, Mississippi, right after graduation. Mound Bayou was a small town of about 1,300 in the **Mississippi Delta,** the floodplain of the Mississippi River. The rich soil of the Mississippi Delta produced good crops of cotton for white landowners. But the African-American families who farmed the land for the white landowners earned very little money.

These sharecroppers pick cotton in the early twentieth century. African-American sharecroppers worked on the large farms of white landowners for very little money.

Every day, Medgar went from door to door selling life and health **insurance** to African Americans. After he made a sale, he went back to that family every week to collect the payment. He had to work late in the evening on his new job. Most of the working men and women who bought the insurance worked all day in the cotton fields. The only time he could talk to them was after they came home.

Sharecroppers

Medgar met many African-American **sharecroppers** who worked on large farms called plantations for white landowners. Sharecroppers did not own their land. They borrowed money from the landowners to buy seed and food to get them through the growing season. After the sharecroppers harvested their cotton, they sold it to the landowners. They also had to give part of the crop to the landowner as rent for the land.

The landowners set the prices for food and supplies at their stores. They also decided how much to pay the sharecroppers for their crops. Most of the sharecroppers and their children had never gone to school, so that did not know how to read or do math. Because of this, they were often cheated by the owners. At the end of the season, most sharecroppers did not earn enough money to pay back the money they had borrowed. They always owed money to the landowners.

Medgar saw how poor they were when he went door to door. The sharecroppers rented shacks without doors and windows from the landowners. Their shacks had no electricity or indoor plumbing. On Sundays Medgar and Myrlie went to visit sharecropper families. They brought old clothes and food. But they could not do much to help. Even though they both worked, they barely earned enough money to support themselves.

Medgar Evers, who was field secretary of the NAACP, is being interviewed for a news program in 1963.

Working for the NAACP

During his first summer in Mound Bayou, Medgar studied the **sharecropping** system. He wanted to find a way to help the families he knew. But the laws favored the landowners. If an African American **accused** a white man of cheating him, the court always decided that the white man was right.

Medgar found a way to make a difference. He joined the **National Association for the Advancement of Colored People**

(**NAACP**). The NAACP was founded in 1909 to fight for the equal rights of all races.

In 1952 only a few people in Mississippi belonged to the NAACP. They were afraid that if they joined, angry whites might take away their jobs or the bank loans for their farms and houses. Medgar told them that the NAACP would protect them. By the end of 1953, more than 1,600 African Americans had joined the new Mississippi State Conference of the NAACP. This was not many in a state with more than a million African Americans, but it was a good start.

A new baby

In June 1953, Myrlie gave birth to a son. Medgar wanted to name him Kenyatta, after an African freedom fighter in Kenya named Jomo Kenyatta. His wife decided this did not sound right for a child in Mississippi. She added the name Darrell. Shortly after the baby was born, she went back to her job as a typist at Medgar's **insurance** company. Medgar's salary was not enough for her to stay home with the baby.

Even with her salary, they could not afford a babysitter. They took the baby to Myrlie's grandmother in Vicksburg, and Myrlie went back to work. Every weekend, Medgar and his wife drove two hours each way to see their baby. Finally, after more than three months, they found a babysitter they could afford. They brought Darrell back to live with them in Mound Bayou.

Thurgood Marshall, a lawyer for the NAACP, later became the first African-American justice of the United States Supreme Court.

Chapter 4:
Medgar Applies to Law School

In 1953 Medgar became the first African American to apply to the all-white law school at the University of Mississippi. Up until then, African Americans could only study in African-American colleges, such as Alcorn State, or at schools in other states. Mississippi law did not allow whites and African Americans to attend the same schools.

There was no separate law school for African Americans in Mississippi, and Medgar did not want to go out of state for his education. He applied to the University of Mississippi. He knew the school would probably not accept him. If that happened, he planned to go to court. He hoped the court would order the school to accept him. He asked Thurgood Marshall, a lawyer for the **NAACP,** to take his court case. Mississippi newspapers printed the story and soon everyone in Mississippi knew that the first African American wanted to attend a white university.

Thurgood Marshall: 1908–1993

Thurgood Marshall was born in Baltimore, Maryland, in 1908. At first he wanted to be a dentist. While he was a student at Lincoln University in Pennsylvania, he decided to study law instead. When he applied to the University of Maryland Law School, he was turned down because he was an African American.

In 1930 Marshall entered the law school at Howard University in Washington, D.C. The school offered new courses in **civil rights** law. Marshall saw that the law might be a good way for African Americans to fight **segregation.** In 1935 when Marshall was 27, he tried his first major case. He represented an African-American student who wanted to attend the University of Maryland law school. Marshall won the **trial** and the student was admitted to the school. This was the same school that had turned Marshall down a few years earlier.

Marshall became a lawyer for the **NAACP** in 1938. He continued to try cases for black students who had been turned down at universities because of their **race.** In 1952 he took a new case that asked the **Supreme Court** to decide if **segregated** public schools were legal. The case was called *Brown v. the Board of Education.* The Supreme Court decided that segregated schools were against the law. This decision gave hope to many African Americans. It also made Marshall famous.

Medgar Evers met Thurgood Marshall at a meeting in Mississippi in the 1950s. When Medgar applied to the University of Mississippi law school, Marshall agreed to take his case if he was turned down because of his race. Medgar was turned down, but he decided not to file a lawsuit.

By 1968 Thurgood Marshall had a successful record as a lawyer. Of the 32 cases he had tried, he had won 29. That year, Marshall became the first African American to serve on the Supreme Court. He served until 1981, when he retired.

In May 1954, the United States Supreme Court, the highest court in the country, ruled that segregation of public schools was against the law. Medgar thought this might help him get into the law school. But months after he sent in his **application,** the University of Mississippi turned him down. An application is a set of forms people fill out, showing why they should be able to go to the school. They told him he did not have enough letters of support from white Mississippians. He knew the real reason: They did not want an African-American student at the university.

A new baby girl

While they were waiting to hear from the University, Medgar's wife found out she was going to have another baby. Myrlie worried about her husband and their family. She knew that angry whites might hurt him for trying to enroll at a white university. That had happened before to African Americans who wanted equal rights. When he was a child, Medgar had seen a black man killed by angry whites. Myrlie also worried that Medgar would not be able to support their growing family if he went back to school. In the end, Medgar decided not to go to court. But Medgar told her that he still needed to fight for a better life for their children.

In September 1954, Myrlie gave birth to a baby girl. They named her Rena Denise Evers.

A new job with the NAACP

In December 1954, when Medgar was 29, he was hired as the **NAACP's** first field secretary in Mississippi. This was their title for the director of all NAACP activities in the area. The family moved to Jackson and he set up an office. Myrlie worked as Medgar's secretary. For the first time in their marriage, they got to see each other all day.

Medgar had many duties. He managed the office, signed up new members for the NAACP, and investigated crimes against African Americans. The NAACP knew Mississippi would be a difficult place to change. NAACP leaders admired Medgar's courage and sense of hope. He believed that most problems could be solved if he worked hard and people worked together.

An end to segregated schools

In 1954 the **Supreme Court** had ruled that **segregated** schools were against the law. But the state of Mississippi claimed that the Supreme Court had no right to tell states what to do. Mississippi did not follow the new ruling. Unless the U.S. government sent soldiers to force them, they would not end **segregation** in the schools. The governor met with African-American leaders and offered to fix up their schools if they agreed to let them stay segregated. The African-American leaders refused. They knew their schools would never get as much money as the white schools.

After the Supreme Court ruled that segregation was against the law, many schools accepted African-American students for the first time. Autherine Lucy (left), was the first African American admitted to the University of Alabama. Here she is leaving the courthouse with her lawyer, Thurgood Marshall in 1956.

In the summer of 1955, Medgar gave speeches all over the state. He explained what the new law against segregated schools meant to African Americans in Mississippi. After each meeting, he passed around a **petition,** a sheet of paper that parents could sign to show that they wanted to end segregated schools. The people who signed these petitions knew that some whites would be angry. It took courage for them to sign.

A smiling Emmett Till is pictured here with his mother in 1955.

In Yazoo City, 53 people signed the petition. The local newspaper printed their names, addresses, and telephone numbers. White people refused to hire the petitioners and stores refused to sell them food. Within a few months, 51 people took their names off the **petition.** The other two moved away.

Murder in Mississippi

In August 1955, a fourteen-year-old African-American boy from Chicago was murdered. Emmett Till was visiting relatives in Money, Mississippi. Back home in Chicago, he was a fun-loving teenager. His mother warned him that the whites in Mississippi would expect him to act like they were better than he was. Even so, when some Mississippi friends dared him to talk to a white woman in the town's grocery store, he agreed. After Emmett bought some candy, he said, "Bye, baby," to the woman. She became very angry.

Three days later, the woman's husband and a friend came to the house where Emmett was staying. It was after midnight. They dragged him out of the house. His body was found in a river several days later. He had been beaten and then shot to death. A heavy fan was tied around his neck to keep his body underwater. When Emmett Till's funeral was held in Chicago, his mother Mable left his casket open. She wanted the whole world to see how her son had died.

Medgar and the **NAACP** investigated the crime, trying to find out what had happened. Finally, the two white men who took Emmett away were arrested. Emmett's relatives agreed to tell their stories in court. Medgar was afraid the **witnesses** would be hurt if they stayed in Mississippi. He planned to get them out of the state after they appeared in court.

Even with several witnesses against them, the killers were found not guilty. Newspapers and television all over the United States reported the **trial.** For the first time, many Americans realized how unfair the laws were in Mississippi.

In 1955 Medgar Evers interviews Mrs. Bulah Melton as part of his work for the NAACP. Mrs. Melton's husband, Clinton Melton, was murdered in Mississippi.

Chapter 5:
The Jackson Movement

Medgar's office in Jackson grew busier every day. African Americans called to ask how to vote, since Mississippi would not let most African Americans vote. Some called to report crimes. Medgar made a written report of every beating and death. When his name appeared in the newspaper, the office received many phone calls from angry whites. Some callers threatened to hurt Medgar and his family. Sometimes, Myrlie was afraid to answer the office phone. But Medgar talked to every caller. He stayed calm, even when the caller was angry.

A new house and a new baby

In 1957 Medgar and his wife built a new house in an African-American neighborhood in Jackson. When they looked at lots for their new home, they liked a large corner lot. But it was too close to the highway. If people wanted to hurt Medgar, they would be able to drive past and get away quickly before anyone saw them. He and Myrlie decided to build on a safer lot between two houses.

As Medgar and Myrlie's children got older, they asked why the parks and swimming pools in Jackson were only for whites. Medgar explained that he and Myrlie were working to change the laws so his children could go to any school or swimming pool they wanted. He told them that African Americans needed to stand up to whites if they wanted change.

When Darrell started school in 1958, Medgar and his wife sent him to a private African-American school. Although the school was **segregated,** it was cleaner and less crowded than the public schools for African Americans. Later, Rena attended the same school. In times of trouble, the teachers protected the children.

In January 1960, Myrlie gave birth to their second boy, James Van Dyke Evers. They called him Van. He was their last child.

The first Mississippi protests

In March 1961, nine African American students from Tougaloo College in Jackson walked into the whites-only public library. They sat down and began to read. They were arrested by the police and taken to jail. The next day, African American students at Jackson State College gathered to **protest** the arrests. To protest is to show publicly that people object to something. They began to march toward the jail. The police fired **tear gas** at them. The gas made them cough and forced them to run away.

James Meredith walks with his lawyer and Medgar Evers (behind) from the Federal Courts Building in 1962. White protesters follow with signs in support of segregation.

In June 1961, the **NAACP** began a program called Operation Mississippi. Its goal was to end **segregation** in the state. As part of the plan, James Meredith, an African-American student at Jackson State University, went to court to enroll at the all-white University of Mississippi. This was the same school that had refused Medgar in 1954. In September 1962, the court ordered the university to accept James Meredith. He went to sign up for classes.

Medgar Evers (center) is arrested for protesting outside a Woolworth's department store in Jackson, Mississippi, in 1963.

Armed guards were sent from Washington, D.C., to protect him from more than 2,000 white **protesters.** While the guards took Meredith inside, the protesters threw rocks. President John F. Kennedy sent an army unit to help police stop the protesters. Two people were killed and more than 160 were injured. But James Meredith became the first African American to attend the University of Mississippi. Medgar finally saw progress.

The Jackson protests begin

In the fall of 1962, Medgar announced a plan. He asked African Americans to stop buying anything from the shops in downtown Jackson. These shops did not hire African-American workers, but they wanted African Americans to spend money there. Medgar also wrote to the mayor of Jackson and asked him to hire African Americans as policeman and fire fighters. The mayor agreed to try. But on May 28, the mayor changed his mind.

That afternoon, three African-American students sat down together at the whites-only section of the **segregated** lunch counter in a downtown store. A group of 200 whites crowded into the store. They poured ketchup and sugar on the students' heads, but the students did not move. One student was dragged off his stool, kicked in the head, and arrested. Seven more demonstrators, including three whites and one Native American, came to the counter and were also beaten. Finally, the manager closed the store. The mob left and friends came to help the demonstrators leave. News of this was shown around the world.

That same night, Myrlie was home alone with their children. After midnight, someone in a car threw a bottle filled with gas at her carport. She heard glass break and soon saw a fire next to the car. She was afraid to leave the house. Someone might be waiting outside to kill her and the children.

Civil Rights Act of 1964

The night that Medgar Evers was killed, President John F. Kennedy gave a speech on television. He spoke about the value of freedom. He said that all Americans should have the right to choose their leaders, their jobs, and their schools. He proposed a new law to protect the rights of Americans of all races and religions.

On July 2, 1964, President Johnson signed the **Civil Rights Act** of 1964. The law said all Americans must be allowed to vote. All Americans had the right to go to public places such as libraries, movie theaters, and sports arenas. It gave all Americans the right to attend any public school. The new law also promised that Americans of every race, color, and religion, and of either sex, would have an equal chance at a job.

Myrlie called a neighbor and asked him to check her front yard. She waited for her neighbor to call back, but she became afraid the gas tank on the car would explode. She ran outside and used the garden hose to put the fire out. Still afraid that she would be shot, she hurried back inside and called the police.

Medgar arrived shortly after the police. Many neighbors and news reporters gathered on the front lawn. Even surrounded by their neighbors, Medgar and his wife knew that their family was in danger. He was becoming very well known.

That spring, the Jackson movement, as it was called, had received inspiration from the Birmingham Movement, led by Dr. Martin Luther King Jr., in Birmingham, Alabama. On May 31, more than 500 African-American students tried to march into downtown Jackson, asking for equal rights. The police stopped them. The police beat them and loaded them into trucks. They took them to the Jackson fairgrounds, because the jail in Jackson was already full of **protesters.** The students were put into dirty animal pens, but they just sang songs about freedom. Some of them were locked up for more than a week.

Medgar worried about the students. He was afraid they might get badly hurt. He talked to their parents and raised money to get them out of jail. On June 1, he and the national executive director of the **NAACP,** Roy Wilkins, joined a picket line protest. They were arrested and jailed. The NAACP headquarters had to send $2,000 to get them out of jail. Most students were released, but the NAACP asked Medgar to discourage the protests. It did not have enough money to get hundreds of students out of jail. The demonstrations the students had planned were canceled. Medgar began to raise money for bail on his own so they could hold more demonstrations. He also encouraged people who would choose jail without bail.

Medgar Evers gives one his last speeches about race relations on television in 1963.

Chapter 6:
Medgar is Assassinated

During May and June of 1963, Medgar often left his house before seven in the morning. People crowded into the office to ask for help. The phone rang constantly. He traveled all over Jackson, meeting with **protesters** and their parents. He skipped many meals because he did not have time to eat. In the evenings, he spoke at meetings in local churches. When he got home, it was usually after midnight.

Medgar was tired, but he was hopeful, too. African Americans in Mississippi were fighting for their freedom. Things were beginning to change. But Myrlie worried about his health and his safety. His face was well known in Jackson from photographs in the newspaper. He also had given a speech on television. Their children gathered around the television each night to listen for their father's name on the news.

After the fire in the carport, Medgar taught his children how to protect themselves. He told them to listen for strange noises. If a dog barked, or if a car stopped in front of the house, he told them to fall to the floor and wait. He asked them where they thought they should hide if someone started shooting at the house. They chose the bathtub. Medgar and his wife were sad and worried that their children were not safe in their own home.

The shooting

On the evening of June 12, 1963, Medgar's wife and children watched President Kennedy give a speech on television. Medgar had called home several times that day to remind his wife about the speech and to talk to the children. He told them he would be home late. The children listened quietly as Kennedy announced the **Civil Rights Act,** a law that would help Americans of every race to vote and receive equal treatment.

Just after midnight, the children heard Medgar's car pull into the driveway. A few moments later, his car door slammed. Then a gunshot rang out. The children fell to the floor and Myrlie ran toward the front door. She switched on the front light and saw Medgar face down on the driveway. Blood soaked the back of his white shirt. He did not move.

Myrlie ran back into the house and called the police. Neighbors who had heard the shot ran toward their yard. They

African-American demonstrators clash with police on June 15, 1963, after a memorial march held for slain civil rights leader Medgar Evers.

In 1964 Byron De La Beckwith, on trial for the murder of Medgar Evers, is handcuffed to a police officer.

turned Medgar over. He was still breathing, but he could not talk. Two neighbors took a mattress and put Medgar on it. They could not wait for an ambulance. They loaded him into a car and took him to the hospital. The children were crying and Myrlie was in shock. A short time later, one of her neighbors came to tell her that Medgar had died. He was 37 years old.

The funeral

More than 4,000 people came to the Masonic Temple in Jackson for Medgar's funeral. Most were black, but some were white. Afterward, most people walked behind the cars carrying the casket to the funeral home. But many African-American young people were angry. They wanted the police to catch Medgar's killer. More than 1,000 of them marched into downtown Jackson. The police stopped them and broke up the march, using police dogs and clubs.

Because Medgar had fought in World War II, he was buried in Arlington National Cemetery in Washington, D.C. Hundreds of people came to the service at his grave. The next day, Myrlie, Darrell, and Rena were invited to meet President Kennedy at the White House. He signed a copy of the new **Civil Rights Act** and gave it to the family.

The trials of Medgar's killer

On June 23, 1963, police arrested a white man for Medgar's murder. Byron De La Beckwith had written many letters to newspapers, arguing in favor of **segregation.** The police found

Myrlie Evers leans over her husband's grave at Arlington National Cemetery in 1964. Her children—Rena, James, and Darrel,—are with her.

Beckwith's fingerprints on the gun that had killed Medgar, and they proved that he owned it. They thought this might be enough to prove that Beckwith had killed Medgar.

The first **trial** began in January 1964. When someone is **accused** of breaking the law, a trial is held to determine whether the person is guilty of a crime. The lawyers chose twelve white men for the **jury.** A jury is a group of people whose job is to decide whether the person is guilty or not. Women were not allowed to serve on juries in Mississippi. African-American men were supposed to be able to serve, but lawyers never chose them. Because no **witness** had seen Beckwith shooting Medgar Evers, the jury could not agree. The first trial ended without a decision.

Beckwith was tried a second time, in April 1964. Again, an all-white jury could not agree, and Beckwith was released. The lawyers decided not try him again unless they had stronger proof.

In the years after Medgar's death, many things changed in Mississippi. African Americans could vote without being afraid they would lose their jobs. Schools were no longer **segregated.** African Americans were chosen for juries. In 1990 a young white lawyer working for the state government in Jackson decided that it was time to investigate Medgar's death again.

In 1994 Beckwith was tried a third time. This time, the jury included eight African Americans and four whites. The government's lawyer had looked at the **evidence** again and found new witnesses. One new witness told the jury that after his first trial Beckwith had bragged about killing Medgar Evers. Another told the jury that she had seen Beckwith's car parked near the Evers' house. With the new evidence, the jury found Beckwith guilty and sent him to prison for the rest of his life.

Myrlie Evers carried on Medgar's work by speaking at rallies like this one at Howard University in 1963.

Chapter 7:
Medgar's Place in History

One year after Medgar's death, Myrlie was invited to the NAACP's national meeting in Chicago. The NAACP honored Medgar with the Spingarn Medal. This award is named for Joel Spingarn, a white educator who served as the chairman of the NAACP in 1914. It is given each year to an African American who has worked for the rights of African Americans. Myrlie accepted the award for Medgar and gave a speech about his life and work.

From that time on, Myrlie spoke to groups all over the United States about Medgar's work for **civil rights.** By talking about his life, she could carry on his name and his work. Her speeches brought a crowd to NAACP meetings. She raised money for the NAACP and helped it sign up new members. In 1964 Myrlie and her children moved to California.

After Medgar was killed, his brother, Charles, became the **NAACP's** new field secretary in Mississippi. Charles had been very close to his brother and was proud to take over his job. In 1969, Charles was elected mayor of Fayette, Mississippi. This was the first time since the 1800s that an African American had won such an election in Mississippi. Charles Evers continued the fight for equal rights that his brother had begun.

Freedom Summer–1964

All over the South, African-American students and their parents were fighting to end **segregation** in the public schools. They were winning, but it took longer in some places than in others. In the summer of 1964, a court ordered Jackson's public schools to accept African-American students in the first grade. Each year, another grade would become **integrated,** which means that whites and blacks would no longer be separated. Medgar's children were too old to be in these integrated classes. But they were proud to see the result of their father's hard work.

In the summer of 1963, the police department in Jackson had hired its first African-American policemen. The waiting rooms at the airport were integrated. After the 1964 **Civil Rights Act,** African Americans and whites in Mississippi could use the same movie theaters, restaurants, hotels, and parks. Many people believed the changes were possible because Medgar and others had worked so hard and had been so brave for so many years. But there was still more left to do.

Supporters cheer as Charles Evers, Medgar Evers's brother, becomes the mayor of Fayette, Mississippi, in 1969.

Dr. Martin Luther King Jr., holds up a photograph of three young civil rights workers, Michael Schwerner, James Chaney, and Andrew Goodman, murdered in Mississippi in 1964 for helping African Americans register to vote.

After Medgar's death, even more African Americans in Mississippi joined the **Civil Rights** Movement. And in 1964, more than 1,000 volunteers, including both black and white students from out-of-state colleges, came to Mississippi to work for civil rights. Some of these students helped African Americans register to vote. But Mississippi was still a dangerous place to work for civil rights. In June three of these students working on voter's rights disappeared. Two of them were white students from New York and one was an African-American student from Mississippi. They were found dead six weeks later. They had been murdered by a group of white Mississippians.

That summer, many students were arrested on false charges, such as disturbing the peace. But the students still managed to sign up more than 80,000 African Americans for the new Mississippi Freedom Democratic Party. Each small success helped to change Mississippi.

Medgar Evers today

In 1970 the City University of New York founded Medgar Evers College in Brooklyn, New York. The college honors Medgar's work by educating students of all races. A Medgar Evers **Scholarship** helps pay for the education of students who show leadership and service to their communities. Alcorn State College in Mississippi also offers a Medgar Evers **Scholarship** to first-year students with good grades.

William Winter, president of the Board of Trustees of the Mississippi Department of Archives and History, watches as Myrlie Evers-Williams signs over the speeches and papers of slain civil rights leader Medgar Evers, April 2002.

In Jackson, a street and a public library have been named after Evers. There is also a life-sized statue honoring him in a public garden. Although Myrlie Evers never moved back to Mississippi, she gave their house in Jackson to Tougaloo College for a museum.

Students from Tougaloo, a private African-American college in Jackson, participated in the **civil rights** marches in Jackson. In April 2002, Myrlie gave Medgar's papers, letters, and tapes of his speeches to the Mississippi State Department of Archives and History. She believes these records belong in his home state.

Two movies have been made about Medgar's life. The first, *For Us, the Living: The Medgar Evers Story,* was made for television in 1983. It is based on Myrlie's book about her life with Medgar. The second movie, *Ghosts of Mississippi,* was made in 1996. It is about Medgar's death and his killer's **trials.** The Evers's house in Jackson was used in the movie.

Medgar did not live to see the changes for which he worked so hard. But he is remembered for his tireless work to bring equal rights to the African Americans of Mississippi. He knew his life was in danger many times. But he was a peaceful man. He never chose violence. He fought with his words.

During Medgar's lifetime, it was easier for African Americans to live in other parts of the United States. Medgar knew that. But he stayed in Mississippi because he loved his home state. He also believed that most of the people there wanted the same rights he wanted. Medgar wanted his children to grow up in a world where they could go to good schools, get good jobs, and vote for anyone they wanted. His work in Mississippi gave them that opportunity.

Glossary

accused when someone says a person has done something wrong

application form people fill out to show why they should be able to go to a school or be hired for a job

civil rights rights that are guaranteed to all citizens by the Constitution of the United States

Civil Rights Act set of laws that ensures Americans of all races and religions have equal rights

evidence proof of what happened

insurance agreement with a company that it will pay for doctor, hospital, or funeral bills. In return, the person who buys insurance makes payments every week, month, or year.

integrate to include all people, regardless of color.

jury group of people whose job is to decide whether a person accused of a crime is guilty or innocent

Mississippi Delta floodplain of the Mississippi River between Vicksburg, Mississippi, and Memphis, Tennessee. The land here is rich but the people who worked on it did not own it and were poor.

National Association for the Advancement of Colored People (NAACP) organization founded in 1909 to promote civil rights for African Americans

petition letter signed by many people who want to change a law

protest to show publicly that people object to something

register sign up to vote in an election

scholarship money given to by various organizations and institutions that helps pay for college costs

segregated organized so that people of different races are apart.

segregation system of rules and laws that kept Southern whites and blacks apart.

sharecroppers people who farmed land they did not own and paid for its use by giving the landowner part of their crops

Supreme Court highest, or most powerful, court in the United States

tear gas strong gas that makes the eyes sting and causes a cough

trial when someone is accused of breaking the law, a trial is held to determine whether the person is guilty or innocent

witness person who gives evidence in a trial

Timeline

1925: Medgar is born on July 2 in Decatur, Mississippi.

1930: Medgar begins school at Decatur Consolidated School.

1933: Myrlie is born March 17 in Vicksburg, Mississippi.

1940: Medgar begins high school in Newton, Mississippi.

1943: Drops out of high school and joins the Army at age 17.

1945: Medgar returns to Decatur after the war.

1946: Medgar attempts to vote, but is turned away by whites.
Returns to finish high school at age 21.

1948: Enters Alcorn State College to study business.

1951: Medgar marries Myrlie Beasley on December 24.

1952: Graduates from Alcorn State College; takes job selling life insurance.

1953: Myrlie and Medgar's first son, Darrell Kenyatta Evers, is born on June 30.
Medgar applies to law school at the University of Mississippi.

1954: Their daughter, Rena Denise Evers, is born on September 13.
Medgar takes job with NAACP in Jackson, Mississippi, in December.
U.S. Supreme Court rules **segregated** schools illegal.

1955: Emmett Till is murdered in Mississippi.

1960: Their last child, James Van Dyke Evers, is born in January.

1963: Medgar is murdered on June 12.

1964: Myrlie moves family to California.
The **Civil Rights Act** is passed.
Mississippi begins to **integrate** public schools.

1994: Byron de la Beckwith is sent to prison for Medgar's murder.

Further Information

Further reading

Altman, Susan. *Extraordinary African-Americans*: From Colonial to Contemporary Times. New York: Children's Press, 2001.

Meltzer, Milton. *There Comes a Time: The Struggle for Civil Rights.* New York: Random House, 2001.

Ribeiro, Myra. *Assassination of Medgar Evers.* New York: Rosen Publishing, 2002.

Turck, Mary C. *Civil Rights Movement for Kids*. Chicago: Chicago Review Press, 2000.

Weber, Michael. *The African-American Civil Rights Movement.* Chicago: Raintree, 2001.

Addresses

Birmingham Civil Rights Institute
520 Sixteenth Street North
Birmingham, AL 35203
Write here to learn about civil rights issues around the world.

Mississippi Department of Archives and History
P. O. Box 571
Jackson, MS 39205-0571
Write here to learn more about Mississippi history.

National Civil Rights Museum
450 Mulberry Street
Memphis, TN 38103
Write here to learn more about the Civil Rights Movement and its impact.

Index